W9-DDO-454

To

From

OTHER HELEN EXLEY GIFTBOOKS INCLUDE:

Sisters! A Little Giftbook
The Love Between Mothers and Daughters
The Love Between Sisters
Go Girl!

OTHER BOOKS IN THIS SERIES:

To my very special Mother
To my very special Daughter
To my very special Friend

This book has been created from the smaller *To a very special*® *Sister* book, which has sold over a million copies and is still one of our strongest sellers. This large-format edition contains a selection of quotes written by Pam Brown, with new illustrations by Juliette Clarke.

To a very special® *Sister* was first published in Great Britain in 1994 by Helen Exley Giftbooks. First published in the USA in 1994 by Helen Exley Giftbooks LLC. This new edition first published in 2007. Copyright © Helen Exley 1994, 2007. The moral right of the author has been asserted.

"To a very special"® is a registered trade mark of Helen Exley Giftbooks.

12 11 10 9 8 7 6 5

ISBN 13: 978-1-84634-181-6

A copy of the CIP data is available from the British Library on request. All rights reserved.
No part of this publication may be reproduced or transmitted in any form or by any means, electronic or mechanical, including photocopy, recording or any information storage and retrieval system without permission in writing from the Publisher.

Illustrated by Juliette Clarke. Written by Pam Brown, copyright © Helen Exley.
Edited by Helen Exley. Printed in China.

Helen Exley Giftbooks, 16 Chalk Hill, Watford, Herts WD19 4BG, UK.

www.helenexleygiftbooks.com

To *my very special* SISTER

WRITTEN BY PAM BROWN
ILLUSTRATED BY JULIETTE CLARKE
EDITED BY HELEN EXLEY

A HELEN EXLEY GIFTBOOK

Simply there

No one thanks sisters or praises
or writes songs about them.

Sisters are simply there
– like one's right arm.

They are totally themselves
– but somehow a part, too,
of one's own life.

Shared lives...

We are linked together by light, invisible chains
– stronger than steel and indestructible.

A sister is always our spiritual Siamese twin...
we are bonded together forever, however separate
our outward lives.

We have our own lives and in some ways
are so very different – but some things we share
– influences, ancestors, experiences, family jokes,
family habits, memories of grief and joy, secrets.
We understand each other a little too well.
We are inclined at times to smile or sigh and say,
"Only she could do a thing like that."

Who greets the news
of your most incredible achievement
with, "Good, I told you
that you could do it."?

You are the person I can't wait to tell good news,

a joke, an adventure, an astonishment.

It's only when I hear you gasp,

hear you giggle, hear you laugh out loud

– only when I see your eyes grow wide

– that the joy's complete.

A sister...

A sister is someone to experiment on,
someone to comfort, someone to scold.
A younger sister borrows just about everything
you possess, and sometimes gives things back.
A sister tells on you to your parents.
A sister accidentally lets out secrets.
A sister gets away with things
you don't or never could. A sister turns to you
when she's in trouble. A sister nags,
tells you to comb your hair, ties up your shoelaces.
A sister says she's too busy to help you
with homework. A sister moans
when she has to take you for a walk.
A sister puts you to bed when you've got 'flu.
An elder sister kisses bruises better.
A sister punches bullies who attack you.
A sister loves you. Most of the time.
Everyone needs a sister.

She accepts me...

How good it is to have someone who accepts me as I am.

A mother's love is a little blind.

A sister's, never.

Sisters know why you are as you are.

Who applauds your successes

– but makes quite sure you don't let them go to your head?

...just as I am

Thank you for hugging me
when all the world went wrong.
Thank you for reading to me when I had measles.
Thank you for blowing my nose
when I was very small.

Thank you for all the last minute repairs –
the standing-up stitchings, the safety-pin anchorings,
the painted-over shoe scuffs,
the nail varnish ladder stops.

Thank you for holding my hand
when I was horribly afraid.

Thank you fo.

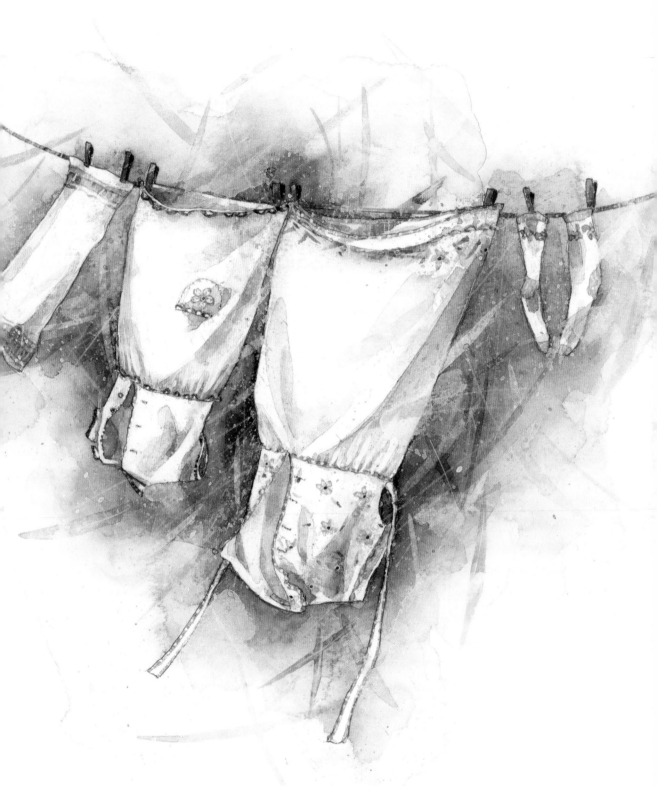

aking care of me

You protected me

In the woods,
you suddenly feel a little hand
take yours
– and you know
you could take on
any dragon
that you chance to meet.

She's more than a friend

Friends we can discard.

Sisters are with us forever.

And so we learn to accept each other as we are.

Good and bad.

Which is the most comforting feeling.

You never really know your friends
– you made their acquaintance too late in life.

Sisters you know.

Siblings are there from the beginning.

We know each other inside out, upside down, bad and good,

with no acted roles, no disguises and no secrets.

We've differed sometimes, and squabbled.

But the link is there forever.

You know who I really am – and accept me.

And forgive me. And are concerned for me.

The way I am for you.

We have something no one in our lives can share

– those years of childhood with their hopes and terrors,

their secrets and their plans.

Only we know what made us as we are today.

Only we remember the small victories and sorrows

for we know the whys and wherefores.

The applause of a sister means far more
than that of any crowd. For she sees your achievement.
She sees all that led up to it.

Sisters know why
you are as you are

YOUR CHIEF DEFENDER

Sisters annoy, interfere, criticize.

Indulge in monumental sulks, in huffs,

in snide remarks. Borrow. Break.

Monopolize the bathroom.

Are always underfoot.

But sisters are your second self.

And if catastrophe should strike, sisters are there.

Defending you against all corners.

When sisters stand shoulder to shoulder,

who stands a chance against them?

Bedlam! Borrowings!
 Stitchings! – Sisters!

Bedlam is a household of sisters

getting ready to go out for the evening.

If your sister is in a tearing hurry to go out
and cannot catch your eye,
she's wearing your best sweater.

Life is never dull with a sister.

Sugar and spice and all things nice.
Perhaps. To an outsider.
…Siblings are more realistic.
To them a sister is naggings and needlings.
Whispers and whisperings.
Bribery. Thumpings. Borrowings.
Breakings. Kisses and cuddlings. Lendings.
Surprises. Defendings and comfortings.
Welcomings home.

Do you remember?

Do you remember whisperings in the dark,

the secrets, the schemes, the gigglings?

And quiet tears. Paddings from bed to bed.

Do you remember our birthdays?

– "I've got a doll, I've got a bear, I've got a harmonica."

Do you remember padding about the kitchen

in the dawn light, getting a Mother's Day breakfast?

The hushing and the clattering and the smell of burning toast.

Do you remember sharing the bath?

The bubbles and the splashings and the wailing

when the soap got in your eyes?

Do you remember falling into the stream?

The scoldings lost in laughter? And the mud.

Do you remember Saturday morning dance class?

Do you remember when the cat had seven kittens?

Do you remember getting lost? And found?

Do you remember the munching of forbidden snacks?

However distant we are from one another,
however life changes us,
we are linked forever.
You will always be a very special part of my life.

...a part of my life

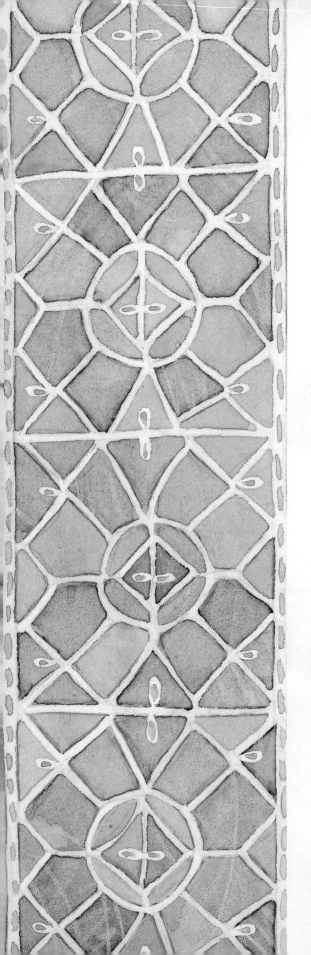

Sisters

Friends are fine.
But for the nitty gritty
family stuff,
one needs a sister.
Like you.

I know that whatever
the disaster I blunder into,
you will rescue me.
Pausing only to tell me
what an idiot I've been.

know it all

Sisters are the best people
to have with you
when you're shopping for clothes.
They tell you the truth.

You can kid the world.
But not your sister.

In troubled times..

Sometimes you just need a hand to hold
– and sisters know when.

You can turn up on a sister's doorstep
at any time and in any state and be sure
of a cup of tea and a listening ear...
And a bed if it's really bad.

Who would I turn to in a dire emergency but you?

When the sky falls in,
a sister will lend you an umbrella.

Remembering
the shared years

Sophisticated sisters, long apart,

can turn into giggly schoolgirls

over just one cup of coffee.

When the dishes have been washed

and the worst of the mess cleared away

("we'll leave the rest till morning"),

sisters kick off their shoes,

loosen their belts and buttons, sprawl in their chairs

and talk and talk. And talk.

Missing you

Your writing on the envelope, your voice on the phone

– and at once I am alert:

"What's happened? What has she done?

Where is she going?"

BROTHERS AND SISTERS
ARE NEVER QUITE ALONE – SO LONG
AS THERE'S A TELEPHONE.

You are just as much my sister

as when we crouched under the table together,

making endless cups of tea for our dolls and teddy bears.

I think of you so much.

Think of me a little.

And phone.

– whatever the distance

Thank you for being there.
How lonely a place the world must be sometimes
for people who have no sisters.

A sister is there – whatever the distance between.

She knows all your loves

Sisters are different. They heard the sobbing
in the darkness. They lived through all your triumphs,
all your failures, all your loves and losses.
They have no delusions.
They lived with you too long.
And so, when you achieve some victory,
friends are delighted
– but sisters hold your hands in silence and shine
with happiness. For they know the cost.

Sisters stand beside you in your hour of triumph
and catch your eye and grin.
They are glad for you – but never dazzled.

all your losses

They know too much about one's past.

They have memories like elephants.

They know one's weak spots.

They are inclined to sigh and say:

"Well – she would, wouldn't she?"

But when one is stuck on a railway station

in the Highlands, or on a road in the country,

when the river has changed course and is running

through the living room,

when one has bumped the car rather badly,

when the boyfriend has just left for good,

when you've all gone down with the 'flu,

when you forgot to order the flowers,

when you have a nasty and persistent pain...

sisters are simply there.

...simply there

When something wonderful happens,
first you phone your partner, then your mother
– and then your sister.
When something appalling happens
– you phone your sister.

Sister in need...
SOS

Often siblings don't see much of each other
once they've grown and gone
– nor do they write or telephone.
But their lives are inextricably entwined
and distance cannot dim their mutual concern.
When trouble comes all sibling rivalry is forgotten
and they give all their energies to comfort,
aid and rescue.

April 5.

˄arg.

please write!

my love ♀

you all
to be any M. Barbosa,
and the Lower Farm,
Nalton St.
...alk

may 21

t me for
lunch 12. o'clock
Sat 26th

. . . .

be a
...k at th
.pub~...
.hi

Thank you for always

Thank you for always being there
– entirely yourself and yet a part of me.

Thank you for being the sort of sister
everyone should have – a companion in adventure,
a sharer of secrets, a lender of hair combs
and sweaters and emergency money.

A friend always.

being there

Together

Talking together brings back those summer skies,

the sweet, high song of larks,

the waist-high grasses. Sweets stuck to their

disintegrating paper bags.

The blank wall chalked with goals and targets.

Alone, it is but half remembered.

Together, we still feel the clutch of each other's hands

as we run from shouting boys or snarling dogs.

Together, we sit at the top

of the darkened stairs and listen to the voices

of the grown-ups.

Together, we are on certain ground.

Even when you are sixty,
you are still six to your sister.

A sister knows
more about you than
anyone else on earth.

Her past is
the same territory as your own.
You both know every path,
every stream,
every turn in the road.

We are part

Until the ending of our days,

we will be part of one another's lives.

However far apart,

however different,

we are essential to each other.

of one another's lives

We share recollections

that no one else can know.

We share sorrows

that none can understand.

We share joys

that are our secret treasure.

Our lives are bound together.

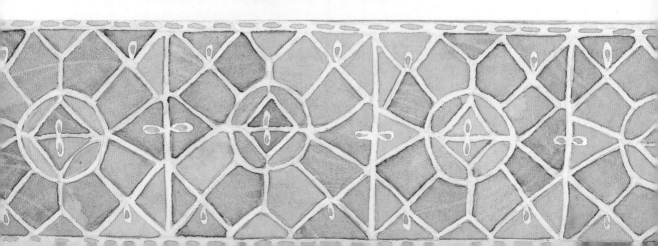

Memories...

We are grown and very different now.

People say – "I would never have taken her for your sister."

But we share the glimmering dark,

birthday cuddles among Mother's pillows

– and the safety of Dad's arms.

We share a secret land where no one else can come.

For we are bound together by a thousand memories.

We shared. Parents. Home. Pets. Celebrations.

Catastrophes. Secrets.

And the threads of our experience became

so interwoven that we are linked.

I can never be utterly lonely,

knowing you share the planet.

I need news of you. I need to know you're safe.

I need you.

Thank you

Thank you for all the things you've lent me.

Thank you for all the things you've sent me,

made for me, shown me how to do.

Thank you for all the rescues, all the cover-ups,

all the scoldings and comfortings.

Thank you for all the laughs,

all the shared adventures.

Thank you for being there for me

whenever I needed you.

You and I were and are and will be forever friends.
Despite all differences. Despite all change.

How very lonely
the world would seem
if one didn't know one's sister
was around somewhere.